SWIFT

A Comprehensive Intermediate Guide to Learn and Master the Concept of Swift Programming

TABLE OF CONTENTS

Introduction

Congratulations on purchasing *Swift: A Comprehensive Intermediate Guide to Learn and Master the Concept of Swift Programming* and thank you for doing so.

Swift is a powerful language that helps one to write great software. The software can be for desktops, servers, iPhones and anything else that can run the code. It is a language that is safe, fast and offers plenty of interaction. It combines the best features of a modern language and other great features from the open-source community. The Swift compiler is created to deliver quality performance. In addition, the language is optimized for development purposes.

Swift is a friendly language to new programmers. It is an industrial-quality programming language that is both enjoyable and expressive. If you write the Swift code in a playground, it gives you the opportunity to test the code and see the results instantly. This saves time of building and running an app. The language defines extensive classes of popular programming errors by borrowing modern programming patterns such as:

- Memory is controlled automatically

- Variables have to be initialized before they are used.

- Checking integers for overflow

- Error handling provides for recovery from unexpected issues

- Checking array indices for out-of-bounds errors

The swift code is compiled and effectively optimized so that it delivers the best performance. Both the syntax and standard library are created depending on the guiding principle of programming. This book provides you with the best lessons as an intermediate or advanced swift developer. The first chapter introduces you to how you can build adaptive user interfaces for your apps. In addition, you learn how to add sections and an index list in the UITableView. The remaining chapters teach you more concepts related to improving the design of your app. Finally, it concludes with how to get direction and draw routes on maps.

Chapter 1

Building Adaptive User Interface

The long story of Apple started with only one iPhone that had a 3.5-inch display. During this time, there was no big deal when it came to designing apps. In fact, you only required to account for two unique orientations. That is the portrait and orientation. After a few years, Apple created an iPad that had a 9.7-inch display. During this period, iOS developers created two different types of screen designs. One was for the iPhone and the other one was for the iPad.

Fast forward to 2018, you will agree that Apple has redefined its products. If you are a lover of Apple products, you must have seen a tremendous change in their devices. With the release of iPhone X, one can actually tell that this giant tech company has invested a lot in creating user-friendly products.

Right now, all iOS developers have a big challenge to develop generic apps that can adapt its User Interface in all Apple's devices and products. Moreover, this is part of Apple's goal to have apps that support any orientation and any iOS device display. Nowadays, apps adapt their UI to a given device and orientation.

This has resulted in a new UI design concept called Adaptive Layout. It started with the Xcode 7, this development tool lets developers create an app UI that can fit in all different devices, screen sizes, and orientation. When you look at the Xcode 8, the interface builder has been further re-defined and streamlined so that it can improve the adaptive user interface. In fact, it comes with a complete full live preview of how things can fit on any iOS device.

New techniques and ideas are involved when it comes to adaptive design. It consists of trait collections, size classes, adaptive fonts, auto layout, etc. Adaptive design helps developers to build universal and localized apps.

If you are an iOS developer, you must be aware of why adaptive design is that helpful. You know how difficult it is to auto-resize masks, keep track of orientations, and develop separate code paths depending on the type of device. Well, the adaptive design seeks to address all these issues.

Size Classes

To achieve an adaptive design, you must know how to use Size Classes. This is one of the most important things that make the adaptive layout a success. Size classes are an abstraction of the way a device is categorized based on the orientation and screen size. By using Size Classes, one is able to remove logic and code that addresses many different kinds of screen sizes, specific devices, and orientations. It further allows one to have a single interface for all devices.

Size Classes exist of two types, regular and compact. Each Size class can be represented both vertically and horizontally. Moreover, each device has its own Size Class, which includes all of its orientations. An iPad, for instance, is usually represented by a regular size class for its large screen.

Compact screen sizes, on the other hand, represent smaller screens, which mean less room. Devices in this size class would include iPhones and iPods. It may vary depending on orientation, however. See the table below:

	Vertically	Horizontally
iPhone Portrait	Regular	Compact
iPhone Landscape	Compact	Compact
iPhone 6 Plus Landscape	Compact	Regular
iPad Portrait	Regular	Regular
iPad Landscape	Regular	Regular

Step 1: Choose a Size Class in the Interface Builder

Proceed to Main.storyboard. The canvas will have a rectangular shape. The bottom of the interface will have "wAny hAny". This means "Any Width, Any Height." This means that anything that is changed on the canvas will affect all Size Classes. You may click on the button, which will show you that you can toggle several different classes.

Step 2: Add an Image

Click on an Image View from the Object Library and drag it towards the canvas. Using the Size Inspector, set the following attributes:

X Position = 0
Y Position = 72
Width = 600
Height = 218

Bring up the Attributes Inspector. Use it to modify the view's mode.

Step 3: Add a label

Bring up the Object Library. Find the label and drag it toward the canvas. Bring up the Size Inspector and set the following attributes:

X position = 16
Y position = 312
Width = 568
Height = 242

Afterwards, go to the Attributes Inspector. Make the following changes:

- Set Alignment to Center
- Set Text to "Silver Laptop"
- Modify the Font Size to System 100.0 points
- Set Lines to 0

Step 4: Adding Constraints

Let's add some constraints for the two objects we've just added.
Next, we want to add constraints for the label and image view. Go to the bottom of the Interface Builder and click Reset to Suggested Constraints located under All Views in View Controller part. In case you see the option greyed out, confirm that one of the views in the canvas is highlighted.

Step 5: Build and Run

At the top of the Xcode, click on iPad Retina so that you can use it for the IOS Simulator. Build and run the app by clicking Command + R. You will discover that the app does fine for the iPad. However, we need to make sure that it works well on any device.

Live Preview

To build and run your app so that you can tell how your user interface works can be tiresome. Fortunately, Xcode 6 has some added ability to allow live rendering of a user interface on any device in any particular orientation. This will allow one to resolve any auto layout problems faster than just running an app in the IOS Simulator every time.

Step 1: Enable Preview Assistant

Move to the top of the Xcode and click Assistant Editor button.
This will split the Xcode's editor into two panes. At the right pane, choose Automatic> Preview > Main.storyboard.

Step 2: Add devices to the Preview

Interface Builder will display a live preview of the user interface on a 4 inch iPhone. You will see that the user interface is less than the actual on the iPhone. If nothing shows up on the preview, click on the view controller located on the left pane to refresh it.

Navigate to the right pane, click the + button found at the bottom so that you can add more devices to the preview. Move on and add the iPad to the preview.

Step 3: Switch Orientations

In the assistant editor, hover your iPhone at the bottom. On the left of the device name, you will see a button, which switches the current orientation. Click it once so that you can switch the iPhone preview to the landscape orientation.

How to install Size Class and Specific Constraints

In case our user interface has some issues, we will require adding some constraints that are specific to a given size of a class. This is another benefit of using adaptive design. We are able to dictate to the user interface how it must lay out its views for specific size classes without adding another storyboard. Initially, it required one to use two different storyboards and load the right one during execution.

Step 1: Image View Base Constraints

First, add constraints that work for most devices and later improve them. Then, remove the constraints that had been added earlier. You do this by clicking any view in the canvas and then you select Editor > Resolve Auto Layout Issues > All Views in View Controller – Clear Constraints.

Choose the image view, click on the Align button, select Horizontal Center in the Container, and finally click Add 1 Constraint. You can then open the Size Inspector on the right and double-click to edit it.

Step 2: Add Label Base Constraints

As a result of the constraints added to the image view, the label already contains the height and vertical spacing from the image view added. Select the label and click the Pin button so that you can add a leading, vertical, and trailing space constraint. Next, if you preview the app in the assistant editor, the constraints make things much better. However, there's a challenge when the app uses a compact horizontal size class.

Step 3: Add a compact Horizontal constraint

Use the size class to toggle the button at the bottom, choose Compact Width, Compact Height. The bar will turn into a shade of blue to show that one is editing the user interface for a particular size class. Select the image view, open the Size Inspector, and update the frame. The next thing you should do is to open the label and update its frame in the Size Inspector.

While you have the label selected and the Size Inspector open, choose the label's constraints and remove it by pressing Delete. You can highlight multiple constraints by long pressing the Shift key. This will remove the constraints added for this Size Class.

Fortunately, Xcode has the ability to tell such constraints. It can either use the image view or selected label. Select Editor > Resolve Auto Layout Issues > All Views in View Controller – and then Reset to suggested Constraints.

Step 4: Preview Updated Constraints

You simply open the Size Inspector for the image view. You will find that there are different constraints listed but some that are greyed out and others aren't. This will show which constraints are active for the present size class.

Try to double-click on any one of them; the bottom part will reveal active classes and constraints.

Chapter 2

Add Section and Index List in the UITableView

An indexed table view represents a more or less plain-styled table view. The only execution is that it contains an index in the right side of the table view. The indexed table is very popular in iOS apps. The most popular examples include the built-in Contacts app on the iPhone. By delivering an index scrolling, users have a chance to access any given section in the table immediately without the need to go through every section.

Below are some of the methods that one will need to know if they want to add sections and index list to the UITableView.

- **NumberOfRowsInsection**: This method will show the total number of rows in a given section.

- **NumberOfSectionsInTableView:** This method shows the sum of sections contained in the table view. Most of the time the number is of the section is set to 1. In case you are interested in having multiple numbers, write a large number.

- **TitleForHeaderInSection**: This method will represent the header titles for different parts. It is an optional method in case you don't allocate section titles.

- **CellForRowAtIndexPath:** This one will return the table data for a given section.

- **SectionIndexTitlesForTableView:** This one returns the indexed titles that show up in the index list on the right side of the view.

- **SectionForSectionindexTitle.** This will display the index section that the table view has to jump when a user touches on a given index.

Demo App

This demo app is a simple app that will display a list of animals in the standard table view. However, this app will place the animals into various sections and offer a list of index list for rapid access. You can look at the image below to understand how the demo app will look.

This chapter focuses on the implementation and index list. It is recommended that if you don't want to build the Xcode from scratch, download online the Xcode template.

How to display Sections in the UITableView

The animal data for this app is stored in the array. What is going to be done is that the data shall be organized into sections according to the alphabetical order. Since it is a demo app, you will replace the animal array with an NSDictionary. The first thing is to define and declare the animals' variable in the NSDictionary. Next, add another array for the section titles using the AnimalTableViewController.m.

```
@interface AnimalTableTableViewController () {
    NSDictionary *animals;
    NSArray *animalSectionTitles;
}
```

Navigate to the ViewDidLoad: method and alter the code. Change it into the following.

```
- (void)viewDidLoad
{
    [super viewDidLoad];

    animals = @{@"B" : @[@"Bear", @"Black Swan", @"Buffalo"],
                @"C" : @[@"Camel", @"Cockatoo"],
                @"D" : @[@"Dog", @"Donkey"],
                @"E" : @[@"Emu"],
                @"G" : @[@"Giraffe", @"Greater Rhea"],
                @"H" : @[@"Hippopotamus", @"Horse"],
                @"K" : @[@"Koala"],
                @"L" : @[@"Lion", @"Llama"],
                @"M" : @[@"Manatus", @"Meerkat"],
                @"P" : @[@"Panda", @"Peacock", @"Pig", @"Platypus", @"Polar Bear"],
                @"R" : @[@"Rhinoceros"],
                @"S" : @[@"Seagull"],
                @"T" : @[@"Tasmania Devil"],
                @"W" : @[@"Whale", @"Whale Shark", @"Wombat"]};

    animalSectionTitles = [[animals allKeys] sortedArrayUsingSelector:@selector(localizedCaseInsensitiveCompare:)];
}
```

11

In this code, the NSDictionary for the animal variable is created. The first letter of the animal is entered as a key. The value that relates with the associated key is the array of the animal names.

Furthermore, the *animalSectionTitles* array has been declared to store the section titles. For convenience purposes, use the keys of the animals in the dictionary to represent section titles. To retrieve the NSDictionary keys, one should call *allKeys: method*. In addition, the titles are sorted in alphabetical order.

The next thing is to modify the *numberOfSectionsInTableView: method* and display the sum of sections.

```
- (NSInteger)numberOfSectionsInTableView:(UITableView *)tableView
{
    // Return the number of sections.
    return [animalSectionTitles count];
}
```

To show the header title for every section, you must implement the *titleForHeaderInSection: method*. Return the section title according to the section index. The next thing is to let the table view understand the number of rows for a given section. Do this by creating the *numberOfRowsInSection: method* while in the AnimalTableViewController.m.

```
(NSInteger)tableView:(UITableView *)tableView numberOfRowsInSection:(NSInteger)section
{
    // Return the number of rows in the section.
    NSString *sectionTitle = [animalSectionTitles objectAtIndex:section];
    NSArray *sectionAnimals = [animals objectForKey:sectionTitle];
    return [sectionAnimals count];
}
```

Once the app begins the rendering process in the table view, the numberOfRowsInSection is called and a new section appears. Depending on the index of the section, one will get the section title and use it as a key to extract the animal names for the section and return the sum of the animal names for a given section. The last thing is to alter the *cellRowAtindexPath: method* as shown below:

12

```
- (UITableViewCell *)tableView:(UITableView *)tableView cellForRowAtIndexPath:(NSIndexPath *)indexPath
{
    UITableViewCell *cell = [tableView dequeueReusableCellWithIdentifier:@"Cell" forIndexPath:indexPath];

    // Configure the cell...
    NSString *sectionTitle = [animalSectionTitles objectAtIndex:indexPath.section];
    NSArray *sectionAnimals = [animals objectForKey:sectionTitle];
    NSString *animal = [sectionAnimals objectAtIndex:indexPath.row];
    cell.textLabel.text = animal;
    cell.imageView.image = [UIImage imageNamed:[self getImageFilename:animal]];

    return cell;
}
```

The index path has the current number of the row plus the current index section. Still, depending on the section index, it is possible to extract the section title and apply it as the key to highlight the animal names for a given section. Once you have done that you can hit the run button to see the result of the app.

If you want to add an index list to a table, you simply need to use a few lines of code. First, add the *sectionIndexTitlesForTableViw: Method* and display an array containing a section index. The section title is used as an index as shown below:

```
- (NSArray *)sectionIndexTitlesForTableView:(UITableView *)tableView
{
    return animalSectionTitles;
}
```

Once you do this you will be done. Try to run the app and see. You should see the index appear on the right side of the table. Surprisingly, no need of implementation and the indexing is fine. Tap any index and you will see a given section of the table.

In case you are working on a large project that you may need to show an extensive record, it will be better to arrange the data into different sections and offer an index list for quick access. This chapter has taught you how to implement the indexed table. So far, you must know how to add sections and index list in a table view using Swift language.

13

Chapter 3

Creating Simple View Animations in Swift

When Apple released iOS 7 and iOS 8, both animation and motion effects turned to be the focus of design both in Apple and other developers of Apple devices. The iOS 7 creates a flat and minimal design to apps. This led to certain apps sharing same UI. To create a difference from other apps, developers use motion effects and animations.

Animations don't just create a unique app but it improves the overall user experience in the application. If you want to see how animations enhance the UX, look at the Apple apps. The Photos app is a great example. If you select a photo from the collection, the photo will expand out and when you close it, it shrinks back to the original photo selected. This further improves the navigation of the app because it will allow a person to know exactly tell where they are if they browsed a collection of photos.

The Facebook's Paper app uses the same animation in a beautiful way to improve the general user experience. In this app, an article is selected by flipping it up. The article will expand out from its thumbnail version, meaning that if you flip the article downwards, it will return to its initial state. In this case, the animation is used to demonstrate how the app operates. If you were interacting with the app for the first time, you would still be able to figure out how to use it without any assistance.

Animations are a great thing. Apart from improving the user experience, animations make users want to continue using the app instead of uninstalling and searching for a better one in the App Store.

There are many different ways of adopting animation in apps. Some of those methods include using a UIKit Dynamic, View controller translations, and layer animations. This chapter examines simple view animations.

This chapter starts with a brief introduction of APIs applied in animating views. In addition, it will present examples of how one can use APIs in the app.

The Basic View Animations

For one to develop animations on views, he or she must change properties on views and allow UIKit to animate it automatically. The properties to change are marked Animatable. The list below shows properties that should be Animatable.

- Bounds

- Alpha

- Transform

- BackgroundColor

- Center

- ContentStretch

All animations include changing one or more of these properties.

When it comes to simple view animations, the UIKit has the following APIs to animate the views on the screen.

- UIView.animateWithDuration(_:,animations:,completion:)

- UIView.animateWithDuration(_:, delay:, options:, animations:, completion:)

- UIView.animateWithDuration(_:, animations:)

The last one accepts two parameters. The first value represents the duration of the animation in seconds and the properties that you want to change. The UIKit accepts the original state of the view and develops a smooth transition from one state to the next based on what one describes in the animation.

The remaining APIs aren't different from the last one but they accept additional parameters that create more configuration to the animation. The first one has a complete closure that one can use to describe another animation which you may want to happen after the first one or perform a cleanup of the UI.

The second API has two additional parameters. That is the delay and options. Delay represents the time one has to wait before the animation begins while UIViewAnimationOptions constant should show how one wants to carry out the animations.

Spring Animations

It models the attributes of a real-life spring. This means that when a view is moved from one point to another, it will shift to the end before finding a position. The method used for spring animations is shown below.

```
UIView.animateWithDuration(_:, delay:,
usingSpringWithDamping:, initialSpringVelocity:,
options:, animations:, completion:)
```

This method resembles the previous method with only two differences.

- The Spring with Damping

- Initial Spring Velocity

Damping refers to a value from 0 to 1 which determines how the view can return to the end of the animation. The near to 1 the value is, the less bouncy it can turn out to be. An initialSpringVelocity determines the initial velocity of the animation. This defines the starting strength of the animation. If you would like it to begin rapidly, then you have to set a large value. However, if you want a smooth animation, then you should set the value to 0.

Keyframe Animations

This will allow anyone to set different stages of the animation. One can group several animations together so that they can share common features but be able to control it individually.

The Keyframe animation APIs is as follows:

- UIView.addKeyframeWithRelativeStartTime(_:,relativeDuration:)

- UIView.animateKeyframesWithDuration(_:,delay:,options:,animations:)

These two methods are used as one with the first one nested in the first animations closure.

The first method will set the general configuration of the animation such as the period it should take, the delay and other options. One can then set one or more of the second method within the animations closure to prepare for the different stages of the animation.

The relative time of start and duration of each frame is a value which ranges between 0 and 1. This value represents the percentage of time in the total duration of the animation.

View Transitions

These transitions are important when you want to add a new view to your view or remove a view from the view hierarchy.

Important APIs that will help you create these view transitions include:

```
UIView.transitionWithView(_:, duration:, options:, animations:, completion:)

UIView.transitionFromView(_:, toView:, duration:, options:, completion:)
```

Use the first view transition to see the view hierarchy. This method accepts parameters the same as the previous animation methods.

The second method helps one to select a view from the view hierarchy and add a new view to its place.

Example

To get started, look for a reference of the constraints that can change. Open the storyboard file and select the constraints.

Chapter 4

JSON and Codable

Codable is one of those great protocols for Swift+. One can use it to encode and decode data formats. For example, JSON to native objects. It is possible for one to map Swift objects to JSON data just by using Codable protocol.

As an iOS developer, you are going to interact with JSON at one point in your life. Every web service right from Facebook to Foursquare uses JSON to fetch data for your app. The question is how can you effectively transform that JSON data into Swift objects?

In this Chapter, you will learn how to work with JSON objects in the Swift language with the help of the Codable protocol. This chapter will further extend into JSONEncoder and JSONDecoder. You will also learn how you can map between JSON and Swift structs.

Importance of Coding and Decoding

Well, what are some of the issues that Codable addresses? Let's study an example.

Assume you are creating a recipe app. This app will display a different list of recipe including instructions, ingredients, and basic information related to food. You receive data associated to the app from the web service as well as their API. This API has the JSON data format.

In brief, JSON is a text-based data format that has many web services including Foursquare, Facebook, and Twitter. Below is an example:

```
{
    "name": "Spaghetti Bolognese",
    "author": "Reinder's Cooking Corner",
    "url": "https://cookingcorner.com/spaghetti-bolognese",
    "yield": 4,
    "ingredients": ["cheese", "love", "spaghetti", "beef", "tomatoes", "garlic"],
    "instructions": "Cook spaghetti, fry beef and garlic, add tomatoes, add love, eat!"
}
```

JSON objects stay inside these brackets {}. Arrays stay inside square brackets [] while property names and strings remain inside quotes. Values can either be strings, arrays, numbers, and objects. However, this is not just interesting; the most interesting thing is that JSON is a great way for one to connect apps and web services.

You see, one of the great things about the internet is the way one can connect many computers in a network. Most of these computers communicate with one another using different protocols such as TCP, SSH, and HTTP. Many of these protocols depend on mutual agreements. The computers can communicate because there is a common language understood by each other.

Websites are created on top of these protocols. When a browser asks for this webpage from the web server, it receives a response that has the HTML format. In this case, the HTML describes the webpage, and then the browser renders it. Once this is done, anyone is able to see and read the page.

So, what has that to do with JSON? This is a format agreed on web services, apps, and APIs. All web apps and online services use it because the format is flexible and simple.

JSON has an amazing capability for one to encode any data format for web services, apps, and APIs. It is used in all online services, web apps because of the simple and flexible format.

JSON has one important ability: one can encode whichever data format in JSON as well as decode it back to any data format. It is this process of decoding and encoding that makes JSON very powerful.

Other data formats such as XML can still be encoded and decoded. JSON is a very popular format for apps and web services. One can select Swift Int, URL, Data, Double and Dictionary values then encode them into JSON. Then send them to the web service that decodes the values into a native format that understands it. Conversely, the web server transfers data encoded as JSON to an app as well as decode the data to native types such as Array and String.

Once the recipe app receives JSON, it's now possible to decode it into Swift struct as shown below:

```swift
struct Recipe {
    var name:String
    var author:String
    var url:URL
    var yield:Int
    var ingredients:[String]
    var instructions:String
}
```

Well, Codable becomes important is the time of encoding and decoding data from native types to different formats. Let's move on and see how it is done!

The Codable Protocol

Previously, to use JSON before Swift 4 was very difficult. One had to serialize the JSON and typecast each property of the JSON to the right Swift type. For example:

```swift
let json = try? JSONSerialization.jsonObject(with: data, options: [])

if let recipe = json as? [String: Any] {
    if let yield = recipe["yield"] as? Int {
        recipeObject.yield = yield
    }
}
```

21

It's hard to deal with possible errors and type discrepancies. While it might work, it's not the right one.

Libraries such as SwiftyJSON simplify the way one works with JSON but one will still require mapping the JSON data into its correct Swift properties and objecting.

However, Swift 4 allows one to use Codable protocol. That means that your Swift class and struct will have to use that protocol, and then you will find JSON encoding and decoding for free.

The Codable protocol consists of two protocols, Encodable and Decodable. Both of these protocols are minimal and seem to define the functions init(from: Decoder) and encode(to: Encoder).

In truth, the JSONDecoder class has code to convert the JSON format into a key-value container so that one can create their own encoder and decoder for any given format. Let's study an example. The first thing is to create a struct called User by doing this way:

```
struct User:Codable {
    var first_name:String
    var last_name:String
    var country:String
}
```

The User struct contains three simple properties of the type String and relates to the Codable protocol. Next, it is to write some bit of JSON. This is the JSON that we shall work with.

JSON data generally enters the app as the response of the web service request. However, in this example the JSON is kept in the JSON string like this:

```
let jsonString = """
{
    "first_name": "John",
    "last_name": "Doe",
    "country": "United Kingdom"
}
"""
```

The next thing to do is to decode the JSON and turn that into a User object. This is how it will look:

- The first thing is to change the JSON string into a Data object by calling the data (String:) function on the string. This is an important step.

- Next is to create the JSONDecoder object and call the decode (_: from:) function on it. This changes the JSON data into an Object of type User through decoding the JSON.

- The next thing is to print the last name of the user using print(user.last_name).

Sounds easy? Basically, you have mapped the JSON object into a Swift struct and decoded the JSON format into a native object that Swift can work with.

Decode with JSON Codable

Let's use the previous example and expand it. This is the JSON to use:

```
let jsonString = """
{
    "first_name": "John",
    "last_name": "Doe",
    "country": "United Kingdom"
}
"""
```

This has to be turned into a Data object.

23

This step is important. Rather than representing the JSON as a string, the JSON is stored as a native Data object. Look into this code and you will realize that it uses force unwrapping to work with the optional return value from data (using:). Next, unwrap the optional more elegantly!

Using this code above, one can respond to errors in case the data (using:) returns nil. One can as well apply the shown error message, or even allow the task to fail and save the diagnostic information in the log.

The next thing is to create a new JSONDecoder object.

Then use this decoder to decode the JSON data.

But the decode (_: from:) function can throw errors. This code will crash when that takes place. Then we can respond to any errors that arise using the code below:

```swift
do {
    let user = try decoder.decode(User.self, from: jsonData)
    print(user.last_name)
} catch {
    print(error.localizedDescription)
}
```

Therefore, the whole code will appear this way. This is how it's different.

The most important thing here is to avoid silencing errors. Just catch the error and respond to it using UX or UI by logging, retrying and fixing the task.

In case the JSON properties such as first_name is not the same with the Swift struct properties, CodingKeys becomes more important.

Each struct and class that is associated with Codable can define a special nested enumeration referred to as CodingKeys. Use it to

24

declare the properties that need to be encoded and decoded plus their names. The User struct in the example below has the property names changed from snake_case to CamelCase.

```
struct User:Codable
{
    var firstName:String
    var lastName:String
    var country:String

    enum CodingKeys: String, CodingKey {
        case firstName = "first_name"
        case lastName = "last_name"
        case country
    }
}
```

If you use this struct together with the previous examples, you will discover that one can use the User object with the new property names.

The CodingKeys is simple to explain. What it does is to map the properties and use the string values to pick the correct property names in the JSON data.

Encode Objects with JSON Codable

Is it possible to encode objects with JSON? Yes. It is done as shown below:

```
var user = User()
user.firstName = "Bob"
user.lastName = "and Alice"
user.country = "Cryptoland"

let jsonData = try! JSONEncoder().encode(user)
let jsonString = String(data: jsonData, encoding: .utf8)!
print(jsonString
```

This is the output of the above code:

```
{"country":"Cryptoland","first_name":"Bob","last_name":"and Alice"}
```

What is going on here?

- The first thing is to define a User object and assign certain values to its properties.

- Next is to use encode (_:) to encode the user objects to a JSON Data object.

- The next thing is to convert the Data object into a String and print it out.

Examine carefully and you will realize that encoding has adhered to the above rules. Still, this example can be expanded so that one can deal with errors.

In this example, the output formatting property is used to encode the "pretty print" in the JSON data. This will create spaces, newlines, and tabs to help make the JSON string easy to read.

Chapter 5

Get Social with Swift

Applying social media features in our apps is not that way easy. Both Apple and Facebook introduced social network capability features, talk of iOS 5 and iOS 6. Before the introduction of these features, developers were required to add a full Facebook and Twitter SDK to facilitate sharing in the apps. Now that it's built in, it is very easy to combine these social features into an app.

To use Social Framework, it facilitates applications to network with other social media from just a single API without the need to handle authentication. Users can log in both to Twitter and Facebook at the OS level in the "Settings" app. This means that a developer doesn't need to go and integrate complete Twitter SDK or Facebook. Everything has been done for you already. It contains a system that provides a view controller for creating posts and an abstraction that permits the use of each social network's API over the HTTP. The Social network framework is a great framework because it offers an interface to network with other social media. With this particular framework, one has to just write a few lines of code to help show up the composer. Then users have an opportunity to publish or tweet a Facebook post on the app.

The social framework has an accessible class called *SLComposeViewController*. This class presents the standard view controller for users to create a tweet and Facebook post. It also permits developers to attach images, preset initial text as well as add URL to the post. When you want to create a simple sharing property, it is the only class that you require.

Let's get started.

The initial Setup

Navigate to the Xcode and click on create a new application. Then click on *SingleViewApplication.*

The next thing is to name the application.

Import Framework

Next, move to the framework section in the Xcode and add another Social Framework to the application. You can check in the image below.

Interface Design

The next thing is to navigate to the interface of the application, where there is a need to add some objects to the view controller. However, the first thing is to create a view.

Below are the instructions to follow.

Move to File> New> Cocoa Touch Class>UIViewController

Name this view controller file as the *SocialViewController*. This is shown in the screenshot below.

Connect the view controller file with the view that will be important in the design and functionality.

Create a connection between variables and Elements

Next is to add some objects to the view controller.

1. The UIView. This will add a custom color to the view. In this example, the Hexa color is used.
2. UILablel. This label helps one write a text so that the design can look elegant.
3. UIButtons. Two buttons will be used so that more actions can be added to it later on.

If you follow everything outlined above. The image below shows how the view will appear.

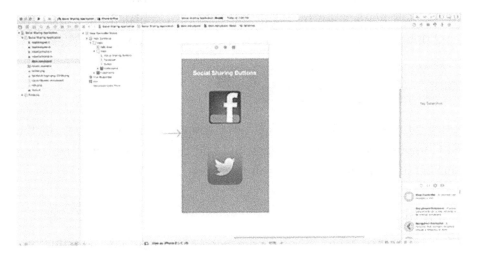

In this image, there are two images added.

To create a link between the objects and view, one has to perform a drag and drop of all objects one by one in the view controller.h file.

- Drag the first Facebook button and create an action using it.

- The next thing is to drag the second Twitter button and create its action. This has been shown below:

```
#import <UIKit/UIKit.h>

@interface SocialViewController : UIViewController

- (IBAction)facebookButton:(UIButton *)sender;

- (IBAction)twitterButton:(UIButton *)sender;

@end
```

Add Facebook Support

In this section, functionality is added to the Facebook sharing feature of the iOS application by using the help of a social framework. The next thing is to add a social framework to the view controller file.

```
#import <Social/Social.h>
```

Once you have done this the next thing is to make use of the SLComposeViewController class and add the view that will facilitate sharing of social media update on Facebook.

Point to note

Make sure that your social media account is configured within the iPhone settings and in case there is no account, there shall be two choices with a custom alert to select cancel or select the settings option.

Twitter Support

This section will illustrate how you can add Twitter functionality and share your social media update by using the twitter button.

Twitter is among the top ways for one to share their feeling and some tweet using twitter. The iOS offers Twitter support by providing the SocialFramework.

1. **First Step**

The first thing is to add the code into the twitter button and use its action to share our tweet on the twitter profile.

Make sure that you first add your personal Twitter details into the Twitter setting within your iPhone. By doing this it will not keep asking you to add the account to it.

2. **Second step**

Add the code below that makes active the function of the twitter button.

```
(IBAction)twitterButton:(UIButton *)sender {

    SLComposeViewController *tweetSheet = [SLComposeViewController
    composeViewControllerForServiceType:SLServiceTypeTwitter];

[tweetSheet setCompletionHandler:^(SLComposeViewControllerResult result) {

    switch (result) {

        case SLComposeViewControllerResultCancelled:

        {

            NSLog(@"Post Failed");

            UIAlertController* alert;

            alert = [UIAlertController alertControllerWithTitle:@"Failed!!" message:@"Something went wrong while sharing
            on Twitter, Please try again later." preferredStyle:UIAlertControllerStyleAlert];

            UIAlertAction* defaultAction = [UIAlertAction actionWithTitle:@"Okay" style:UIAlertActionStyleDefault
            handler:^(UIAlertAction * action) {

            }];
```

```
    [alert addAction:defaultAction];

    dispatch_async(dispatch_get_main_queue(), ^{

        [self presentViewController:alert animated:YES completion:nil];

    });


    break;

}

case SLComposeViewControllerResultDone:

{

    NSLog(@"Post Sucessful");

    UIAlertController* alert;

    alert = [UIAlertController alertControllerWithTitle:@"Success" message:@"Your post has been successfully
    shared." preferredStyle:UIAlertControllerStyleAlert];

    UIAlertAction* defaultAction = [UIAlertAction actionWithTitle:@"Okay" style:UIAlertActionStyleDefault
    handler:^(UIAlertAction * action) {}];

        [alert addAction:defaultAction];

        dispatch_async(dispatch_get_main_queue(), ^{

            [self presentViewController:alert animated:YES completion:nil];

        });

        break;

    }

    default:

        break;

    }

});

[self presentViewController:tweetSheet animated:YES completion:Nil];

}
```

This will work in the same way a Facebook code operates. It will display success or failure status when updating the status.

Add image to the post

When you want the post to have an image. The process is quite simple. All you require to do is to write a single line of code and leave the rest to be done independently.

This will use the tweet sheet image sharing the property that one can use to add the custom image inside it.

By using this code, it will help a developer to add an image to the post. Don't forget to add an image to the asset folder before you can call it using this code.

For those who don't know how they can create a custom alert of their choice. You can use the method below. The alert view is outdated and in its place, there is going to be an alert controller that has the updated code in regard to the Apple's guidelines.

The first thing is to create an alert controller object and link the message, title and alert type to it. The next thing is to add an alert action that can perform an action once a user clicks on any given object action. Lastly, add the action inside the alert controller object and display the view using the presentViewController method.

If you follow each step outlined here, you will have created an application that can help you share your social status on the social media networks without going to use API. Nowadays, it is very easy to integrate Twitter and Facebook when you choose to use Social Framework in iOS 6. In case, you are creating an app, there is every reason why you should use it. It will add value to your app and boost your popularity.

```
public func font(forTextStyle textStyle: UIFont.TextStyle) -> UIFont {
    guard let fontDescription = styleDictionary?[textStyle.rawValue],
        let font = UIFont(name: fontDescription.fontName, size: fontDescription.fontSize) else {
            return UIFont.preferredFont(forTextStyle: textStyle)
    }

    let fontMetrics = UIFontMetrics(forTextStyle: textStyle)
    return fontMetrics.scaledFont(for: font)
}
```

To use it with the *Noteworthy.plist*, load it in the controller:

Chapter 6

Send SMS AND MMS in Swift language

The Message UI framework is not designed for email purposes but it also delivers specialized view controller for developers to submit a standard interface to compose SMS text message in the apps. While one uses the MFMailComposeViewController class for the email. This same framework facilitates MFMessageComposeViewController to deal with a text message.

Generally, how the MFMessageComposeViewController is applied is the same as the mail composer class. Don't worry because this section will go through the MFMessageComposeViewController class so that you can understand how to use it.

A demo app

This app will show a list of files in a table format. However, rather than presenting the main composer, the app will display a message on the interface with a pre-populated message content any time a user touches on any table rows.

Let's get started

To save time from the need to create the Xcode project, get a template to start to code. However, a new programmer of iOS SDK, you are advised to create the project from scratch. There are various programming tutorials that one can depend on to learn more from the table view as well as the storyboard.

Import Message UI Framework

The first thing to do is to import the MessageUI framework into the project.

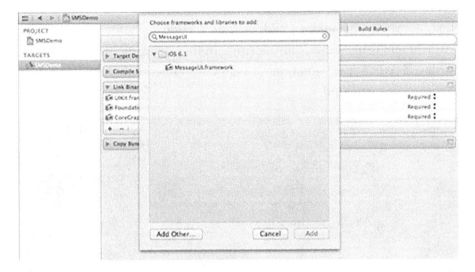

How to implement the Delegate?

Navigate to the "AttachmentTableViewController.m" then add the code below to the import MessageUI header and implement the MFMessageComposeViewControllerDelagate.

```
#import <MessageUI/MessageUI.h>

@interface AttachmentTableViewController () <
MFMessageComposeViewControllerDelegate>
```

The MFMessageComposeViewControllerDelagate protocol declares a single method that can be called anytime a user completes composing an SMS message. There is a need to deliver the implementation method that can deal with different situations.

1. The user cancels SMS editing.

2. The user touches on the send button and the SMS is sent and delivered successfully.

3. The user touches on the send button but there is no SMS send.

Next, you should add the code below to the "AttachmentTableViewController.m". In this stage, an alert message is displayed when the situation 3 happens. Other cases, the message composer is dismissed.

```
(void)messageComposeViewController:(MFMessageComposeViewController *)controller didFinishWithResult:(MessageComposeResult)
result
{
    switch (result) {
        case MessageComposeResultCancelled:
            break;

        case MessageComposeResultFailed:
        {
            UIAlertView *warningAlert = [[UIAlertView alloc] initWithTitle:@"Error" message:@"Failed to send SMS!"
            delegate:nil cancelButtonTitle:@"OK" otherButtonTitles:nil];
            [warningAlert show];
            break;
        }

        case MessageComposeResultSent:
            break;

        default:
            break;
    }

    [self dismissViewControllerAnimated:YES completion:nil];
}
```

Creating the Message Composer

If a user clicks on any of the rows, the selected file is retrieved and call a custom method to show up the message composer. Update the "didSelectRowAtindexPath:" method using the code below:

```
- (void)tableView:(UITableView *)tableView didSelectRowAtIndexPath:(NSIndexPath *)indexPath
{
    NSString *selectedFile = [_files objectAtIndex:indexPath.row];
    [self showSMS:selectedFile];
}
```

The key method here is the "showSMS:" method that initializes and populates the default content of the SMS text message. Add the code below:

```
(void)showSMS:(NSString*)file {

    if(![MFMessageComposeViewController canSendText]) {
        UIAlertView *warningAlert = [[UIAlertView alloc] initWithTitle:@"Error" message:@"Your device doesn't support SMS!"
        delegate:nil cancelButtonTitle:@"OK" otherButtonTitles:nil];
        [warningAlert show];
        return;
    }

    NSArray *recipents = @[@"12345678", @"72345524"];
    NSString *message = [NSString stringWithFormat:@"Just sent the %@ file to your email. Please check!", file];

    MFMessageComposeViewController *messageController = [[MFMessageComposeViewController alloc] init];
    messageController.messageComposeDelegate = self;
    [messageController setRecipients:recipents];
    [messageController setBody:message];

    // Present message view controller on screen
    [self presentViewController:messageController animated:YES completion:nil];
}
```

Although many of the iOS devices should have the ability to send a text message, being a programmer you have the role to facilitate an exception. Assume if the app is used with an iPod touch that has the iMessage disabled. In such a situation, one can be sure that the device cannot send a text message. Therefore, at the start of the code, the device has to be verified to make sure that it can send a text message using the "canSendText" method in the MFMessageComposeViewController.

The remaining code is easy to understand. One can pre-populate multiple recipients phone numbers in the text message. For instance, the message body allows only textual content alone.

When the content is ready, call the "presentModalViewController:" to show up the message to the composer.

Time to compile and run the app

Once you have done all these, you are good to go. It is time to run the app and see the results. However, make sure that you test the device on a real iOS device. A simulator cannot permit one to send SMS.

Suppose you don't prefer in-app SMS

The previous implementation delivers a seamless integration of the SMS feature in the app. But let's assume that you only want to redirect to the default Messages app and send a text message. It becomes more simple. You can achieve that in a single line of code.

37

```
[[UIApplication sharedApplication] openURL: @"sms:98765432"];
```

In the iOS, an individual is allowed to communicate with other apps with the help of the URL. The mobile OS comes with the built-in support of the HTTP, tel, mailto and SMS URL schemes. In case you open the HTTP URL, the default iOS launches the URL using Safari. If you are interested in opening the Messages app, use the SMS URL schedule and describe in detail the recipient. But these schemes of URL don't support one to show up the default content.

Chapter 7

Custom Fonts and Dynamic Type

Custom font and dynamic type took time and effort before it was scaled for each text style when a user changes the dynamic type size. Apple created a new font metrics class in iOS 11 that made it easy and simple. It reduced the pain that previously existed.

The Dynamic Type

This was introduced by Apple in the iOS 7 to present a user with a system-wide mechanism to convert the desired text size from the system settings. To facilitate the use of Dynamic type, one has to define labels, text views and text fields to a specific font presented by UIFont class method called preferred font(forTextStyle:). The font returned has the Apple San Francisco typeface. This contains both size and weight modified for the user's size preference and the desired text style. For instance, to build a label that has the body text style:

```
let label = UILabel()
label.font = UIFont.preferredFont(forTextStyle: .body)
label.adjustsFontForContentSizeCategory = true
```

Some notes

- Apple created the adjustsFontForContentSizeCategory property to UITextField, UILabel and UITextView in the iOS 10. If it is true, the font will automatically be updated when the user alters the required font size. In case of iOS 9 and other earlier versions, one should listen for the

39

UIContentSizeCategoryDidChange notification and update the font manually.

- The iOS 10 also provides one with a font that is compatible with the size class using the preferred font (forTextStyle: compatibileWith:).

- There are six UIFontTextStyle values that have been introduced in the iOS 7(. subheadline, body,. caption1, .footnote, caption2). There are four more styles added by iOS 9 (. title1, title2, title3 and. callout). iOS 11 adds the large style title(. largeTitle).

Below, you can look at how the different styles appear at extra small, large and accessibility extra-extra-extra-large sizes.

Title 1	Title 1	
Title 2	Title 2	**Title 1**
Title 3	Title 3	
Headline	Headline	**Title 2**
Subheadline	Subheadline	
Body	Body	**Title 3**
Callout	Callout	
Footnote	Footnote	**Headline**
Caption 1	Caption 1	Subheadline
Caption 2	Caption 2	Body
		Callout
		Footnote
		Caption 1
		Caption 2

Pay attention in the way all the text styles increase in size with accessibility. This is a new feature in iOS 11. Remember. Larger accessibility sizes introduced in iOS 7 are applied to the body style alone.

Scale A Custom Font

Before the release of iOS 11 that supported the dynamic type using a custom font, an individual was supposed to change the details of the font for every ten text styles and determine how to scale the font choices for each of the twelve content size categories.

Apple releases the font metrics used for the San Francisco typeface in the iOS Human Interface Guidelines. This is an important starting point that helps one to decide how they can scale each text style.

For instance, the. headline text style has a Semi-bold face that has 17 pt with the large content size and 23 pt at the xxxLarge size.

Font Metrics

To simplify the processing of scaling a custom font for the dynamic type, Apple introduced the UIFontMetrics in the iOS 11. To make use of a custom font for a specific text style, one has to first get the font metrics for each style and use it to scale the custom font.

Let's go back to the example of setting a label to the body text style but using a custom font. The correct action to take is as follows:

```
let font = UIFont(name: fontName, size: fontSize)
let fontMetrics = UIFontMetrics(forTextStyle: .body)
label.font = fontMetrics.scaledFont(for: font)
```

The font is developed using a custom font face and size. Look for the font metrics of the. body style and apply the scaledFont(for:) to receive the font scaled of the preferred text size.

The UIFontMetrics class eliminates the need to have a table of fonts for every twelve content size category. Still, you require to choose on a font for every style at the default content size.

Style Dictionary

To prevent the scenario of scattered names and sizes through the code, this example has a style dictionary that contains the face name and size applied at each of the styles at the. large content size. To reduce the complexity of customization as well as changing the typefaces. The style dictionary has been kept in a plist file.

This is the way it appears in the Noteworthy typeface that Apple bundles using iOS. It contains both a bold and light face.

Key	Type	Value
▼ Root	Dictionary	(11 items)
▶ UICTFontTextStyleTitle0	Dictionary	(2 items)
▶ UICTFontTextStyleTitle1	Dictionary	(2 items)
▶ UICTFontTextStyleTitle2	Dictionary	(2 items)
▶ UICTFontTextStyleTitle3	Dictionary	(2 items)
▼ UICTFontTextStyleHeadline	Dictionary	(2 items)
fontName	String	Noteworthy-Bold
fontSize	Number	17
▶ UICTFontTextStyleSubhead	Dictionary	(2 items)
▼ UICTFontTextStyleBody	Dictionary	(2 items)
fontName	String	Noteworthy-Light
fontSize	Number	17
▶ UICTFontTextStyleCallout	Dictionary	(2 items)
▶ UICTFontTextStyleFootnote	Dictionary	(2 items)
▶ UICTFontTextStyleCaption1	Dictionary	(2 items)
▶ UICTFontTextStyleCaption2	Dictionary	(2 items)

In this example, the. large font size for apple text size has been used for every style. For example, a 17 pt Noteworthy-Bold of the. the headline and a 17 pt Noteworthy-Light for the. body.

To use the fonts, one has to wrap the dictionary into a ScaledFont utility class which one has to initialize with the name of the plist file. The font(forTextStyle:) method shows a scaled font for every style.

```
public final class ScaledFont {
    public init(fontName: String)
    public func font(forTextStyle textStyle: UIFontTextStyle) -> UIFont
}
```

Look at the code for the complete details but there is an interesting way which searches for the font for each text style and applies the UIFontMetrics to show the scaled font. In case the style dictionary does not contain an entry for the text style, it will use the Apple preferred font:

```
private let fontName = "Noteworthy"

private lazy var scaledFont: ScaledFont = {
    return ScaledFont(fontName: fontName)
}()
```

Then when you want to set the font for a label, you call the font(forTextStyle:)

```
let label = UILabel()
label.font = scaledFont.font(forTextStyle: textStyle)
label.adjustsFontForContentSizeCategory = true
```

When the font is scaled using UIFontMetrics, the property called adjustsFontForContentSizeCategory will continue to work. This means there will be no need to worry about updating when the user changes the size. This is how it will appear in the Noteworthy font.

Title 1	Title 1	Title 1
Title 2	Title 2	Title 2
Title 3	Title 3	Title 3
Headline	**Headline**	**Headline**
Subheadline	Subheadline	Subheadline
Body	Body	Body
Callout	Callout	Callout
Footnote	Footnote	Footnote
Caption 1	Caption 1	Caption 1
Caption 2	Caption 2	Caption 2

Custom Font

There are no restrictions to apply the typefaces in the iOS. Remember. This is NotoSans extracted from google fonts. It contains regular, italic, bold and bold-italic faces. The italic has been used both for the subheadline and caption styles.

Title 1	Title 1	Title 1
Title 2	Title 2	Title 2
Title 3	Title 3	Title 3
Headline	**Headline**	**Headline**
Subheadline	*Subheadline*	*Subheadline*
Body	Body	Body
Callout	Callout	Callout
Footnote	Footnote	Footnote
Caption 1	*Caption 1*	*Caption 1*
Caption 2	*Caption 2*	*Caption 2*

If you want to download and add custom font files into your project, it is important to remember to add them into the target and arrange them under the "Fonts provided by application" key in the Info.plist:

▼ Fonts provided by application ⇕ ⊕ ⊖	Array	⇕ (3 items)
Item 0	String	NotoSerif-Regular.ttf
Item 1	String	NotoSerif-Bold.ttf
Item 2	String	NotoSerif-Italic.ttf

If you are not sure which font names to apply, use the code below with all the variable names in the code snippet:

```
let families = UIFont.familyNames
families.sorted().forEach {
    print("\($0)")
    let names = UIFont.fontNames(forFamilyName: $0)
    print(names)
}
```

Override the iOS Dynamic Type font family

The recent releases of iOS allow Dynamic Type. This is a great system for one to add accessible typography in the app. Choosing to use a Dynamic Type lets the user define a system-wide font size that can then be reflected in the app. The Dynamic Type supports different predefined text styles such as footnotes, titles, and captions that one can use to change the typographical salience of the content.

This marketing approach makes it look great but one is left surprised why not every app supports it. But the Dynamic Type has a huge drawback. For one to make an app unique from the rest, one should use the custom fancy-pants font. However, this is not permitted by the Dynamic Type.

Modify Font Descriptors

By using the UIFontDescriptor class, one can get some type of specification for every font. The descriptor shall codify the information such as weight, font family, style and font name. To get a descriptor from a font is very easy: one basically selects it from the fontDescriptor property of the UIFont. To change the descriptor to the original font, you pass an argument to the UIFont constructors.

The target here is to pick a font instance build by Dynamic Type and change the font that has a custom family name but still maintains all the other properties. This is not easy because it can change the font family name of a descriptor. Therefore, the font is reset. In addition, if the font descriptor is selected and a few changes are done, the final outcome is a font descriptor that has some properties which override the custom font family in other occasions.

This requires one to be smart. The first thing is to extract the required font traits and create a new font descriptor from nothing and detail the precise traits that are required. This is shown in this code snippet:

```
// Get a font from Dynamic Type
var font = UIFont.preferredFont(forTextStyle: UIFontTextStyleHeadline)

// Our overridden font family name
let newFamilyName = "Avenir Next"

// Extract the weight
let weight = (font.fontDescriptor.object(forKey: UIFontDescriptorTraitsAttribute)
    as! NSDictionary)[UIFontWeightTrait]!

// Create a new font traits dictionary
let attributes = [
    UIFontDescriptorTraitsAttribute: [
        UIFontWeightTrait: weight
    ]
]

// Create a new font descriptor
let descriptor = UIFontDescriptor(name: font.fontName, size: font.pointSize)
    .withFamily(newFamilyName)
    .addingAttributes(attributes)

// Find a font that matches the descriptor
font = UIFont(descriptor: descriptor, size: font.pointSize)
```

The global font family overrides appearance proxy

The method presented above is still powerful and one is supposed to set the fonts manually everywhere. The code can be altered into a computed property that an individual can define globally using the UIAppearance proxy protocol. This is shown below:

```
{
    var fontFamily: String {
        get {
            // Extract the font family from the current descriptor. This is not really
            // necessary but provides a sane value for the required getter.
            return font.fontDescriptor.object(forKey: UIFontDescriptorFamilyAttribute)
                as! String
        }

        set {
            // Extract the weight
            let weight = (font.fontDescriptor.object(forKey: UIFontDescriptorTraitsAttribute)
                as! NSDictionary)[UIFontWeightTrait]!

            // Create a new font traits dictionary
            let attributes = [
                UIFontDescriptorTraitsAttribute: [
                    UIFontWeightTrait: weight
                ]
            ]

            // Create a new font descriptor
            let descriptor = UIFontDescriptor(name: font.fontName, size: font.pointSize)
                .withFamily(newValue)
                .addingAttributes(attributes)

            // Find and set a font that matches the descriptor
            font = UIFont(descriptor: descriptor, size: font.pointSize)
        }
    }
}
```

By using a single line of code, one can automatically override the font family of the UILabel instances in the app while still retaining the font style and size from the Dynamic Type. Simply add the line below into the application delegate class:

```
UILabel.appearance().fontFamily = "Avenir Next"
```

When you have this line, one can configure the labels to use a predefined Dynamic Type Class for the best accessibility as well as enjoy a typographical fanciness of a custom font.

Chapter 8

Create Better iOS Animations

Animations are important in creating a unique user experience. They serve various needs and purposes including catching the attention of the user and directing their actions to results on the screen.

Animations further develop a unique experience for the app user. Animations support a specific level of responsiveness and interaction that is not possible in other areas. To develop better animations, one is supposed to create a sense of connection between the user interaction and visual changes. One of the ways that you can achieve this is to develop complete interaction in animations.

The importance of Interactive Animations

Interactive animations existed from a long time ago since the release of the first iPhone. The first appearance of the original iPhone was the "slide to unlock" screen, in this version the user had to directly move the slider before he or she could unlock the device. This specific type of animation was intuitive to those that had never used a multi-touch device.

Interactive animations allow a user to have freedom over the user interface. A direct manipulation is one of the natural interaction models most importantly on mobile devices. It integrates the actions to on-screen animations and provides complete control over a cancellation of the actions.

Furthermore, it appears great, users are able to relate an app the way it looks and how better it works. Therefore, when it appears great, they will pardon other issues with the app. This chapter will guide you on how to create interactive popup animation using Swift language.

UIViewProprtyAnimator

This property was added to the UIKit in the iOS 10 and upgraded in the iOS 11. It delivers a UIView-level object-oriented API to build animations. If you use a traditional UIVIew animation, you will need to write something close to this:

```
UIView.animate(withDuration: 1, delay: 0, options: [.curveEaseOut], animations: {
    self.myView.transform = CGAffineTransform(translationX: 50, y: 0)
    self.myView.alpha = 0.5
}, completion: nil)
```

However, if you are to use the UIViewProprtyAnimator, this is how you are going to write.

```
let animator = UIViewPropertyAnimator(duration: 1, curve: .easeOut, animations: {
    self.myView.transform = CGAffineTransform(translationX: 50, y: 0)
    self.myView.alpha = 0.5
})
animator.startAnimations()
```

This code resembles the UIViewPropertyAnimator, first, you need to develop an animator object and call startAnimation() rather than call a static method on the UIView class.

UIViewPropertyAnimator is very useful when the animation increases in complexity. Before going to look at the code, it is necessary to study the state machine backing UIViewPropertyAnimator.

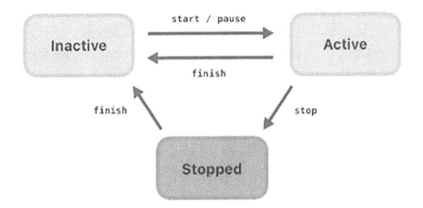

An animator can assume any of the above three possible states. That includes active, inactive and stopped. An animator is defined and initialized while in the inactive state but it will change to an active state when it is paused or started. Once the animation is complete, it goes back to the inactive state. When a started animation is paused, it continues to be in the active state and it can't go through a state transition.

Let's look at how you can apply the UIPanGestureRecognizer plus the UIViewPropertyAnimator to create an animation.

```
var animator = UIViewPropertyAnimator()

private func handlePan(recognizer: UIPanGestureRecognizer) {
    switch recognizer.state {
    case .began:
        animator = UIViewPropertyAnimator(duration: 3, curve: .easeOut, animations: {
            myView.transform = CGAffineTransform(translationX: 275, y: 0)
            myView.alpha = 0
        })
        animator.startAnimation()
        animator.pauseAnimation()
    case .changed:
        animator.fractionComplete = recognizer.translation(in: myView).x / 275
    case .ended:
        animator.continueAnimation(withTimingParameters: nil, durationFactor: 0)
    default:
        ()
    }
}
```

Please note that the pauseAnimation() has to be called instantly after the startAnimation(). Since this animation starts on a pan gesture, chances are that the user will want to scrub the animation first before they can release their touch. If the animation is paused, the fraction completed property is set to shift the view along with the user's touch.

Attempting to do this using the standard UIView animations, more logic will be required than what is shown in the above code snippet. The UIView animations don't have a simple way that one can directly take charge of the completion percentage of the animation or even permit one to pause and resume the animation to the end.

A popup Menu

This section shall teach you how to create a complete interactive, scrubbable, interruptible and reversible popup menu. There are 10 steps to follow. To make everything simple, all the views are created and modified in the code, even though this code can still operate with views build in the storyboard. Furthermore, the code will be inside the ViewController. Swift file.

1. Touch to open and close

The first thing is to make the popup view animate the states between open and close. No fancy additions are done here, simply use the basics of UIViewProperty Animator.

```swift
private enum State {
    case closed
    case open
}

extension State {
    var opposite: State {
        switch self {
        case .open: return .closed
        case .closed: return .open
        }
    }
}

class ViewController: UIViewController {

    private lazy var popupView: UIView = {
        let view = UIView()
        view.backgroundColor = .gray
        return view
    }()

    override func viewDidLoad() {
        super.viewDidLoad()
        layout()
        popupView.addGestureRecognizer(tapRecognizer)
    }
```

```swift
        transitionAnimator.addCompletion { position in
            switch position {
            case .start:
                self.currentState = state.opposite
            case .end:
                self.currentState = state
            case .current:
                ()
            }
            switch self.currentState {
            case .open:
                self.bottomConstraint.constant = 0
            case .closed:
                self.bottomConstraint.constant = 440
            }
        }
        transitionAnimator.startAnimation()
    }

}
```

```
private var bottomConstraint = NSLayoutConstraint()

private func layout() {
    popupView.translatesAutoresizingMaskIntoConstraints = false
    view.addSubview(popupView)
    popupView.leadingAnchor.constraint(equalTo: view.leadingAnchor).isActive = true
    popupView.trailingAnchor.constraint(equalTo: view.trailingAnchor).isActive = true
    bottomConstraint = popupView.bottomAnchor.constraint(equalTo: view.bottomAnchor, constant: 440)
    bottomConstraint.isActive = true
    popupView.heightAnchor.constraint(equalToConstant: 500).isActive = true
}

private var currentState: State = .closed

private lazy var tapRecognizer: UITapGestureRecognizer = {
    let recognizer = UITapGestureRecognizer()
    recognizer.addTarget(self, action: #selector(popupViewTapped(recognizer:)))
    return recognizer
}()

@objc private func popupViewTapped(recognizer: UITapGestureRecognizer) {
    let state = currentState.opposite
    let transitionAnimator = UIViewPropertyAnimator(duration: 1, dampingRatio: 1, animations: {
        switch state {
        case .open:
            self.bottomConstraint.constant = 0
        case .closed:
            self.bottomConstraint.constant = 440
        }
        self.view.layoutIfNeeded()
    })
```

The correct animation code is within the popupViewTapped function called after the view is tapped. So what one has to do is create an animator, assign animations to change the value of a constraint and begin the animator.

A state enum is introduced to show if the popup is closed or open. In addition, there is a computed opposite property that displays the opposite of the current state. This can also be implemented using a boolean flag, but it is very easy to reason about once the animation code turns complex.

One of the most important things to highlight is that the value of the constraint is manually getting updated when the animation ends. This has to be automatically done using the animator, however, if you could fix it explicitly then you could repair some edge-case bugs.

2. Adding a pan gesture

To make an animation interactive, there is a need to introduce a second gesture recognizer. This allows the user to begin and interrupt the animation by swiping over the popup view.

```
@objc private func popupViewPanned(recognizer: UIPanGestureRecognizer) {
    switch recognizer.state {
    case .began:
        animateTransitionIfNeeded(to: currentState.opposite, duration: 1.5)
        transitionAnimator.pauseAnimation()
    case .changed:
        let translation = recognizer.translation(in: popupView)
        var fraction = -translation.y / popupOffset
        if currentState == .open { fraction *= -1 }
        transitionAnimator.fractionComplete = fraction
    case .ended:
        transitionAnimator.continueAnimation(withTimingParameters: nil, durationFactor: 0)
    default:
        ()
    }
}
```

This code resembles the previous example with just one difference. This supports interruption of the animation. As you can see, the animation code has been refactored into a function called animateTransitionIfNeeded that drives the rest of the code that was initially inside the popuViewTapped function.

3. Record the progress of the animation and fix the interruption offset

A problem arises when an animation is interrupted, that is it shifts away from the user's touch. This is as a result of the panhandler not handling the current progress of the animation. To solve this problem, there is a need to record the fraction completed by the animator and use it as the baseline when one calculates a pan offset. A property will be required to record the current progress of the animation.

```
private var animationProgress: CGFloat = 0
```

Once the pan gesture assumes its starting state, one can begin to record the current progress of the animation.

```
animationProgress = transitionAnimator.fractionComplete
```

In the pan gesture's changed state, one has to add the animation progress to the calculated fraction.

55

```
transitionAnimator.fractionComplete = fraction + animationProgress
```

So now the pan gesture works correctly and monitors the user's finger in a natural way.

4. Introduce custom instant pan gesture

The interruption behavior works in a rather surprising manner. For the pan to get recognized, it is important for the user to touch the screen and move their finger in any given direction. One would like the action to be that of a scroll view that permits users to catch the view once they tap down. As per the moment, both the tap gesture plus pan gesture get triggered by touch up. To activate an event on the touchdown, one can create a personal custom gesture recognizer. The code is shown below:

```
class InstantPanGestureRecognizer: UIPanGestureRecognizer {
    override func touchesBegan(_ touches: Set<UITouch>, with event: UIEvent) {
        if (self.state == UIGestureRecognizerState.began) { return }
        super.touchesBegan(touches, with: event)
        self.state = UIGestureRecognizerState.began
    }
}
```

The above is a pan gesture subclass that goes to the begin state on the touchdown. It permits one to replace all the earlier gesture recognizers. The tap has become instant and ends immediately it starts. Making a choice to use this custom gesture recognizer, can enhance the behavior of the earlier tap solution so that the logic can be simplified.

5. Use pan velocity to reverse animations

There is only one problem that is yet to be solved. The popup does not follow the direction the view is "thrown". Once you tap on the closed popup, and capture its mid-animation and then swap back down, it will proceed to animate open. To solve this issue, one has to reverse the animator. This will depend on several factors some of which include the present state of the popup if the animator is currently reversed as well as the velocity of the pan gesture.

Therefore, the ended incidence of the pan gesture handler shall appear this way:

```
let yVelocity = recognizer.velocity(in: popupView).y
let shouldClose = yVelocity > 0
if yVelocity == 0 {
    transitionAnimator.continueAnimation(withTimingParameters: nil, durationFactor: 0)
    break
}
switch currentState {
case .open:
    if !shouldClose && !transitionAnimator.isReversed { transitionAnimator.isReversed = !transitionAnimator.isReversed }
    if shouldClose && transitionAnimator.isReversed { transitionAnimator.isReversed = !transitionAnimator.isReversed }
case .closed:
    if shouldClose && !transitionAnimator.isReversed { transitionAnimator.isReversed = !transitionAnimator.isReversed }
    if !shouldClose && transitionAnimator.isReversed { transitionAnimator.isReversed = !transitionAnimator.isReversed }
}
transitionAnimator.continueAnimation(withTimingParameters: nil, durationFactor: 0)
```

This logic can appear hard to understand but you can figure it out by taking into consideration all other possible cases. In the changed incident of the pan gesture handler, one is supposed to pay attention to the isReversed property of the animator.

```
let translation = recognizer.translation(in: popupView)
var fraction = -translation.y / popupOffset
if currentState == .open { fraction *= -1 }
if transitionAnimator.isReversed { fraction *= -1 }
transitionAnimator.fractionComplete = fraction + animationProgress
```

So far, the animation is reversed. If a user would like to close the popup mid-animation, it is easy for them to achieve that.

6. Corner radius animation

In the iOS 11, there is a CALayer's corner radius that is Animatable without the need for a CABasicAnimation. This implies that one can update the view's corner radius in the animation block and still it will work fine.

```
self.popupView.layer.cornerRadius = 20
```

It is also possible to define the corners around. In the following case, the top left and top right corners are the ones that need rounding.

57

```
view.layer.maskedCorners = [.layerMaxXMinYCorner, .layerMinXMinYCorner]
```

So far, the top two corners have been animated besides the original animation.

7. Improve its elegance

The gray popup view works better, however, some visual improvements make it look better. You can add a background image as the overlay view, a subtitle shadow, title label, and sample reviews.

8. Label animation

There is no built-in method that one can animate a label's color or the font style. The way is achieved is through a simple workaround. To make the transition smooth, one is supposed to animate the scale and translation of every label so that it can overlap in the whole length of the animation.

9. Refactoring for multiple animators

This label animation will operate correctly, however, one could improve the timing so that the transition becomes more smooth. To alter the timing curve of the label animations, you require extra animators. That is the UIViewPropertyAnimator which has one timing curve. This means that for one to use multiple curves, it is a must to integrate multiple animators.

It is important to refactor the code a little so that one can support several animators. To achieve this one, an array of animators is created as shown below:

```
private p var runningAnimators = [UIViewPropertyAnimator]()
```

Once a new animator is created, it is added to the array of running animators.

```
runningAnimators.append(transitionAnimator)
```

When the animation ends, one can remove it from the array. To enable the remaining code to work with the multiple animators, anything that is going to be used on the transitionAnimator has to be applied to the whole array.

10. Create new animators for the alpha label

With the new infrastructure, one can create two new animators to animate the new label in and another one to animate the old label out. The advantage of having multiple animators is that everything has its own timing curve.

```
let inTitleAnimator = UIViewPropertyAnimator(duration: duration, curve: .easeIn, animations: {
    switch state {
    case .open:
        self.openTitleLabel.alpha = 1
    case .closed:
        self.closedTitleLabel.alpha = 1
    }
})
inTitleAnimator.scrubsLinearly = false
```

In this example, the animator's scrubsLinearly property is set to false to make the fraction completed of the animation to be mapped to the ease-in timing curve. In general, animations which emulate the finger of the user should assume a linear timing curve. And that is the reason why this property is true by default.

The difference is small but it will permit the animation to get customized further in the near future. Ensuring that one gets this transition right is essential when the user has complete control over the animation and can also scrub it to a given point.

59

Chapter 9

Create a today widget in Swift Language

The most popular feature in iOS 8 is the ability to develop different types of extensions. This Chapter will take you through the process of building a custom widget for the Today section notification center. First, you will get to learn some few topics related to the extensions and learn important topics about widgets.

Definition of an extension

An extension refers to a unique binary. Don't confuse it with a complete app because it still requires a containing app as a distribution. This may be an existing app that has one or more extensions. Even though extensions aren't distributed independently, it has its own container.

The extension is activated and controlled in the host app. It might be a Safari if you are building a share extension or even a Today system app that manages notification and other widgets. Every system area that allows extension is referred to as an extension point.

To build an extension, one is supposed to develop a target to the project of the containing app. The templates that exist in the Xcode have the right frameworks for every extension point. This allows the app to interact with and stick to the right policies of the host app.

The Today extension

Extensions that have been built for today extension point are referred to as widgets. These have been developed to supply a simple and quick access to information. The widgets connect to the Notification Centre framework. Every developer is advised to design a widget using a simple and focused user interface because a lot of interaction can create a problem. You should also know that you don't have access to a keyboard.

Widgets are meant to perform well and ensure that the content remains updated. Performance is an important aspect that should be considered. A widget is supposed to be available quickly and make use of resources in the best way possible. This will prevent bringing down the whole experience. The system stops widgets that have excess memory. It is important that a widget is simple and focused towards the content it displays.

Let's now create a custom today widget. The widget that is being created will display information related to disk usage as well as a progress bar to deliver a fast visual experience for the user. There are also other important concepts of the iOS 8 extensions that shall be covered.

The Target Setup

1. Setting up the Project

When you want to create a widget extension to an app that is already existing, navigate and open the Xcode project and go straight to the second step. However, if you are beginning from scratch, then you have to start by building a containing app.

To create a containing app, open the Xcode and go to the File menu. In the file menu, click New > Target.

While in the iOS tab, select the "Today Extension "template then click next. Fill the Product Name and choose the correct "Embed in Application" Target.

In the Extension Target General Tab, you can decide to set the Version as well as the Build so that it matches the main iOS of the project to prevent the warning below from arising.

"CFBundleVersion Mismatch and CFBundleShortVersionString Mismatch"

Remove Storyboards

In case you don't want to use storyboards, you can choose to delete the "MainInterface. Storyboard" file. Starting from Info.plist, you can go to the NSExtension directory and delete the NSExtensionMainStoryboard key. Add a new key to the NSExtension dictionary named "NSExtensionPrincipalClass" and select the main "ViewController.swift" which matches the NCWidgetProviding protocol.

You can also add @objc(ViewController) tag to the top of the View Controller class to prevent any error such as "Terminating app due to uncaught exception 'NSInvalidArgumentException', reason: '*** setObjectForKey: object cannot be nil".

Import Pods

If you want to apply cocoa pods in the widget, you can add the new widget target into the Podfile plus a new target. The example below will show the SnapKit pod to the "TodayExtension" widget.

```
target 'TodayExtension' do
    platform :ios, '9.0'
    use_frameworks!
    pod 'SnapKit', '~> 3.2.0'
end
```

Create the View

One can still apply the auto layout to develop the today widget view. The width of this widget is constant. The today widget comes compact both in size and contains a fixed height of 110pts. However, the user can still click "Show More" on the widget so that they can expand and "show less" to minimize it. While in the show more state, the widget can contain variable height that extends to the screen size.

If you want to know when the user has altered the display mode, you can implement the function below:

```
func widgetActiveDisplayModeDidChange(_
activeDisplayMode: NCWidgetDisplayMode,
withMaximumSize maxSize: CGSize)
```

It is possible to check the active display mode and retrieve the maximum width and heights present. In case you are in the expanded state, you can make use of the. expanded rather than. compact.

Entitlements

When you want to share data between the today widget and the host application, you might need to add the "App Groups" entitlement. Go to the project and navigate to your widget's Target and choose the Capabilities Tab. Switch on the App Groups and add a new App Group using a unique name such as "group.com.domain.app". Navigate to the container application's Capabilities and activate the App Groups, choose the same app group that you had created earlier.

Now you can share the data between the two apps by using a UserDefaults suite name.

The Custom URL

In case you would like to tap on the Today Widget or even open the container/host application, then you must be ready to create a custom URL scheme. Simply follow the first step and register the custom URL scheme.

Chapter 10

UICollectionView Custom Layout

The UICollectionView exists from iOS 6. It is a popular UI element to all iOS developer. The reason why it is such an amazing resource is that it separates data and presentation layers. This depends on a different object to manage the layout. The layout is then responsible for defining the placement and visual attributes of the views.

There is a great chance that you might have applied the default flow layout that exists in the UIKit. This contains a normal grid layout plus a few customizations. However, one can organize the views in whichever way they want, this tends to make the collection view powerful and flexible.

This chapter will take you through the process of creating a layout that is similar to the Pinterest app.

The Pinterest app contains a gallery of photos. With the app, you are able to browse the photos. The gallery has been created with the help of a collection view that has a standard layout.

Create a custom collection view layout

The first thing to do when you want to develop a stunning collection view is ensuring that you have a custom layout class for the gallery. The collection view layouts include subclasses of the abstract UICollectionViewLayout class. This often defines the visual properties of each item in the collection view. The individual features represent the instances of the UICollectionViewLayoutAttributes and it has properties of every item in the collection view. That includes the item's transform and frame.

Develop a new file in the Layouts group. Click Cocoa Touch Class by navigating to the iOS\Source list. Assign it the name Pinterest layout and create a subclass of the UICollectionViewLayout. You should ensure that the language used is Swift before you can create the file.

The next thing is to develop a collection view that can use a new layout. Click the Main.storyboard and choose Collection View while in the Photo Stream View Controller Scene. This is shown in the figure below:

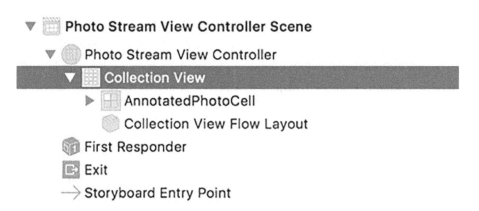

The next thing is to open the Attributes Inspector and choose Custom while in the Layout drop-down list. Here you can move on and click PinterestLayout while in the Class drop-down list.

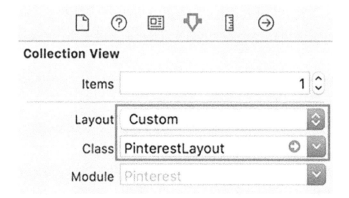

Collection View

Items   1

Layout   Custom

Class   PinterestLayout

Module   Pinterest

Then you can build and run to get a look at how it will appear.

Core Layout Process

Take some time and consider the collection view layouts process that is a combination between the layout object and collection view. Anytime the collection view requires information related to the layout, it will request the layout object to deliver specific methods in a given order.

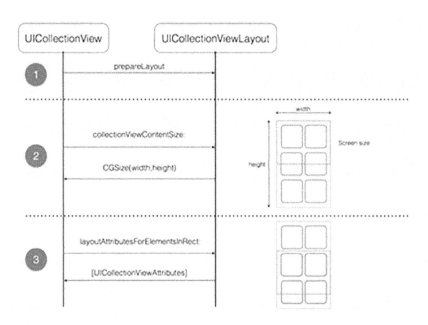

The layout subclass has to implement the following methods:

1. Prepare (): This method is applied when a layout operation is going to take place. It is the role of the developer to perform the calculations needed to define the collection view's size as well as the position of the items.

2. CollectionViewContentSize: This method will present the width and height of the collection view's contents. One has to override it and return the width and height of the whole collection view's content. The collection view has internal information that can be used to configure the scroll view's content size.

3. LayoutAttributesForElements(in). This method requires one to return an attribute of layout for every item in the rectangle. The attributes are returned to collection view in form of an array of UICollectionViewLayoutsAttributes.

4. LayoutAttributesForItem(at): This method offers a high demand layout information to the collection view. One is supposed to override it and go back to the layout attributes for all the items that have been requested by the indexPath.

How can you calculate the attributes?

To calculate attributes for this particular layout, one has to dynamically calculate the height of each item because nobody knows what the height of the photo can turn out to be. One has to declare a protocol that will supply information to the Pinterest layout when it wants.

To return to the code. First, you should open Pinterest layout.swift and add the protocol declaration below before the Pinterest layout class.

```
protocol PinterestLayoutDelegate: class {
  func collectionView(_
  collectionView:UICollectionView,
  heightForPhotoAtIndexPath indexPath:IndexPath) ->
  CGFloat
}
```

In this code, PinterestLayoutDelegate protocol is declared. It has a
method that asks for the height of the photo. This protocol is
implemented in PhotoStreamViewController.

There is just one thing that one can do before they can implement the
layout methods. An individual has to declare some properties that will
be important to the layout process. To achieve that, add the code below
to the Pinterest layout:

```
weak var delegate: PinterestLayoutDelegate!

// 2
fileprivate var numberOfColumns = 2
fileprivate var cellPadding: CGFloat = 6

// 3
fileprivate var cache = [UICollectionViewLayoutAttributes]()

// 4
fileprivate var contentHeight: CGFloat = 0

fileprivate var contentWidth: CGFloat {
  guard let collectionView = collectionView else {
    return 0
  }
  let insets = collectionView.contentInset
  return collectionView.bounds.width - (insets.left + insets.right)
}

// 5
override var collectionViewContentSize: CGSize {
  return CGSize(width: contentWidth, height: contentHeight)
}
```

68

This code has certain properties defined that one will require to supply information to the layout. This is explained below step-by-step:

1. It maintains a reference to the delegate
2. There are two properties that help one configure the layout. The cell padding and a number of columns.
3. It is an array where calculated attributes are cached. Once you call prepare(), you need to calculate the attributes for every item and add it to the cache. When the time comes for the collection view to ask for the layout attributes, one is supposed to be efficient and query the cache rather than recalculate each time.
4. It declares two properties for the content size. The contentHeight is increased when photos are added, and the width of the content is calculated depending on the collection view width.
5. It overrides the CollectionViewContentSize method that returns the size of the collection view's contents. One can apply both the contentHeight and contentWidth from other steps to help calculate the size.

Now you can start to calculate the attributes of the collection view items that will comprise of the frame. Take a look at the following diagram to help you understand how to do it.

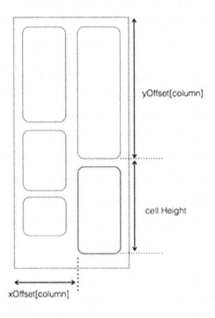

So you will need to calculate the frame of each item depending on the column offset and the position of the earlier item that is monitored by yOffset.

If you want to calculate the horizontal position, you have to begin with the X coordinate of the column item and then add a cell padding. The vertical position represents the starting point of the previous item in the column and height of the previous item. The height of the general item is the sum of content padding and image height.

This is done to prepare (). Add the method below to the Pinterest layout:

```
override func prepare() {
  // 1
  guard cache.isEmpty == true, let collectionView = collectionView else {
    return
  }
  // 2
  let columnWidth = contentWidth / CGFloat(numberOfColumns)
  var xOffset = [CGFloat]()
  for column in 0 ..< numberOfColumns {
    xOffset.append(CGFloat(column) * columnWidth)
  }
  var column = 0
  var yOffset = [CGFloat](repeating: 0, count: numberOfColumns)

  // 3
  for item in 0 ..< collectionView.numberOfItems(inSection: 0) {

    let indexPath = IndexPath(item: item, section: 0)

    // 4
    let photoHeight = delegate.collectionView(collectionView, heightForPhotoAtIndexPath: indexPath)
    let height = cellPadding * 2 + photoHeight
    let frame = CGRect(x: xOffset[column], y: yOffset[column], width: columnWidth, height: height)
    let insetFrame = frame.insetBy(dx: cellPadding, dy: cellPadding)

    // 5
    let attributes = UICollectionViewLayoutAttributes(forCellWith: indexPath)
    attributes.frame = insetFrame
    cache.append(attributes)
```

```
    // 6
    contentHeight = max(contentHeight, frame.maxY)
    yOffset[column] = yOffset[column] + height

    column = column < (numberOfColumns - 1) ? (column + 1) : 0
  }
}
```

Let's explain the above code based on the numbered comments

1. The layout attributes are calculated only when the cache is empty and the collection view exists.

2. It declares and populates the xOffset array using x-coordinate for each column depending on the width of the column. The yOffset array shall monitor the y-position for each column. Then you can initialize every value in the yOffset to 0.

3. This will rotate around all items existing in the first section since this layout has one section.

4. The frame calculations happen here. Width has been calculated previously and cell padding between cells omitted.

5. This builds an instance of the UICollectionViewLayoutAAttribute. Then it defines the frame with the help of the insetFrame and joins the attributes to the cache.

71

6. In this line, the contentHeight is expanded to make up for the frame of the newly calculated item. It will then expand the yOffset of the current column depending on the frame. Lastly, it expands the column so that the next item is placed inside the column.

The most important thing to remember is that while prepare () is called, there are a lot of cases in a normal implementation where one may require to calculate the attributes. So you will require to override layoutAttributesForElements(in). This is what the collection view calls after prepare() to define elements that are visible in a specific rect.

Add this code at the end of the PinterestLayout:

```
override func layoutAttributesForElements(in rect: CGRect) -> [UICollectionViewLayoutAttributes]? {

    var visibleLayoutAttributes = [UICollectionViewLayoutAttributes]()

    // Loop through the cache and look for items in the rect
    for attributes in cache {
        if attributes.frame.intersects(rect) {
            visibleLayoutAttributes.append(attributes)
        }
    }
    return visibleLayoutAttributes
}
```

Here one is supposed to iterate through the attributes in the cache and confirm whether the frames intersect with the rect. Then you can add any type of attributes with frames that intersect with the rect to layoutAttributes. Eventually, this is returned back to the collection view.

The last method that needs to be implemented is the layoutAttributesForItem (at:)

```
override func layoutAttributesForItem(at indexPath: IndexPath) -> UICollectionViewLayoutAttributes? {
    return cache[indexPath.item]
}
```

In this case, you will need to retrieve and go back to the cache layout attributes that are similar to the requested indexPath.

Before you get to see how the layout operates, you require to implement the layout delegate. PinterestLayout depends on this to create photo and annotation heights when you want to calculate the heights of an attribute frame.

Now, open the PhotoStreamViewController. Swift and add the extension below to the end of the file so that it can accept the PinterestLayoutDelegate protocol.

```
extension PhotoStreamViewController: PinterestLayoutDelegate {
  func collectionView(_ collectionView: UICollectionView,
                  heightForPhotoAtIndexPath indexPath:IndexPath) -> CGFloat {

    return photos[indexPath.item].image.size.height
  }
}
```

Lastly, add the code below inside viewDidLoad (), it should be below the super:

```
if let layout = collectionView?.collectionViewLayout as? PinterestLayout {
  layout.delegate = self
}
```

This will set the PhotoStreamViewController to be the delegate for the layout.

Finally, you can build and run the app to see how the cells get positioned and sized depending on the heights of the photos.

Chapter 11

Get Directions and Draw routes in Swift

Directions and Draw routes in Swift

This chapter will guide you on how to draw a route map on the Mapkit between two points using Swift language. You will use MKAnnotation's to draw the pins for source and destination. To get the route, one has to use MKDirection class and create a polyline on the MkMapView. Use the steps below to help you learn how you can draw a route between places on the MKMapView.

1. Create a fresh project called 'DrawRouteOnMapKit'. Navigate to the "Main.storyboard" and drag the 'Map Kit view' to the view.

2. While on the "ViewController. Swift", develop an IBOutlet of the map kit view.

3. Open 'Main.storyboard' and create a link between the mapkitview in the first step.

4. Next, open the 'ViewController. Swift', this is the time you need to develop a class for the pins. Also, MKAnnotations will act as a pole for the source and destination location.

5. Now that you have created a custom class successfully for the pin. This is the time to determine direction between two locations and draw a route on the Mapkit. Go to the

ViewDidLoad, then create coordinates for the source location and destination location.

6. Next is to use a custom MKAnnotation class and develop pins for the source and destination locations using coordinates defined in the last step.

7. If you choose to build and run the app at this point, two points will show up on the map.

8. To get the direction for routes between two points, you must develop a placemark with the help of the MKPlaceMark class that accepts coordinate. Two placemarks for the source and destination location will be created.

9. To find the directions, use the MKDirectionRequest class. The MKDirectionRequest class has features such as the destination, transportType and source. Finally, use the MKDirection class and determine the directions. You will receive directions in the callback. Here is the final code. Build and run the app so that you can see the pins without a route. Therefore, you will need to create a delegate method for the MapKit to help you render the route.

10. Define the delegate of the mapview to self and implement the delegate method.

Conclusion

You have successfully completed Swift for Intermediate Programmers. You have learned how to build adaptive user interfaces for your iPhone apps. So far, you know how to animate table views in cells. You don't have to worry when it comes to JSON and Codable in swift because you know what to do and how you can do it. All the way, you have covered different things related to creating apps in Swift.

Until now, you can combine most of the features learned in this book and develop a Swift application. Besides that, you can apply your own knowledge and understanding to write some simple iOS applications and Mac OS X applications.

Programming in Swift language is by far the most exciting thing. As you may realize, Apple had several reasons to build and launch this language for the iOS platform. One of the reasons is to help new developers approach their platform with some ease and increase both the stability and safety of their applications. Therefore, as a Swift developer, you can be sure that you will build apps that are safe and secure. Think of Swift as a scripting language that has both the elements of functional programming and object-oriented programming.

That said, it is important to know that you have just started. Keep moving forward. Don't stop here. Get other advanced Swift books and expand your knowledge of Swift programming. Remember. This book has only covered major areas in Swift app design. There are still plenty of topics that you need to master.